The Legend
of
NED KELLY

The Legend
of
NED KELLY

Australia's outlaw hero

Paintings by Sidney Nolan

Text by Robert Melville

Introduction by Alan Moorehead

A STUDIO BOOK

The Viking Press · New York

© THAMES AND HUDSON LONDON 1964
THE NED KELLY PAINTINGS © SIDNEY NOLAN
PUBLISHED IN 1964 BY THE VIKING PRESS INC.,
625 MADISON AVENUE, NEW YORK 10022, N.Y.
LIBRARY OF CONGRESS CATALOG CARD NUMBER: 64-25702
PRINTED IN FRANCE BY INTERGRAPHIC

LIST OF PLATES

The paintings are a uniform size of 36 × 48 inches, and are painted in ripolin on hardboard. Acknowledgements are due to the Museum of Modern Art and Design of Australia, Melbourne, and to Clive Turnbull, Melbourne.

INTRODUCTION

Until quite recently there has been no great stirring in the arts in Australia. Since Melba's clear and beautiful voice first emerged out of the cockney twang in the 1890's, the country had to wait half a century for a soprano with the talents of Joan Sutherland. The best of Australian writers, such as Henry Lawson and Henry Handel Richardson, hardly rose to the first flight. Neither sculpture nor architecture found much support in a young colony struggling for survival, and the theatre for the most part relied on importations from abroad. A school of naturalistic landscape painters was at work in the early years of this century, and some, like Arthur Streeton and Penleigh Boyd, achieved distinction, but that was all.

None of this is to be greatly wondered at: after all, the first white settlers arrived in the country barely a century and a half ago; they had to labour for existence in a wilderness, and even now the entire population hardly exceeds that of London or New York City. In a good climate the enjoyment of sport, rather than art, was the natural course of things. Australia's record, in short, has been rather like that of the American Middle West, a region it much resembles.

Soon after the Second World War, however, it became apparent that a fresh wind was blowing. A group of young novelists appeared, presently a good play came along—Ray Lawler's *Summer of the Seventeenth Doll*—and a new generation of poets began to look for something beyond the bush ballads that had once been the mainspring of Australian poetry. In painting there was an especially interesting development: the work of men like Russell Drysdale and William Dobell had a detachment that was a decided break from the imitative canvases of the past. And with the emergence of Sidney Nolan it seems possible that Australian painting has achieved a definite emancipation.

Nolan, despite all evidence to the contrary, is an Australian of the Australians. He has evoked his talent in harmony with the peculiar environment of the country. Factory worker, farm hand, cook, sign painter, odd-jobman—he has been all these things. He knows poverty and the crowded back streets of new cities as well as the immense horizons of the outback. The descendant of Irish immigrants, none of whom had any connection with art, Nolan was born in 1917 in the working-class district of Carlton, in Melbourne, and grew up in the shadow of the financial depression, which was particularly hard on a new country where hardly anyone had resources of any kind. He left school at the age of fifteen and took jobs where he could find them. Painting—he began to attend life classes before he was sixteen—reading and the writing of poetry (he has been almost as much poet as painter at times), were preoccupations that he had to pursue on the side and often at night. All this is typical of the struggle every sensitive and intelligent Australian boy had in a materialistic environment that turned to beer, betting and sport for relaxation, and rejected as "soft" and probably bogus any pretensions to culture or art.

But the essence of Nolan's Australian-ness goes a good deal deeper than this, for he possesses to the full that sense of nostalgia, of bereftness, of isolation, which up to now has been at the root of the Australian approach to life. The paintings on these pages are, to some extent, Nolan's expression of the incompleteness; and in expressing it he conquers it.

Let me be a little more explicit. Australians of my generation grew up in a world apart. Until we went abroad we had never seen a beautiful building, hardly ever heard a foreign language spoken or been to a well-acted play, or eaten a reasonably sophisticated meal, or listened to a good orchestra; and outside the two or three art galleries in Melbourne and Sydney, there was scarcely a house that contained a collection of worthwhile paintings. Nor were any of these matters much talked

viii

about. This was not absolutely a cultural vacuum, for we had books (Australians per head are among the greatest readers in the world), magazines, gramophone records, prints, and, on another level, the movies and the radio. The trouble with all these things was that they were importations, and inevitably any strivings that we ourselves made towards the intellectual and artistic life were, very largely, an imitation of those importations from abroad. Australian women dressed themselves according to European fashions, and the well-to-do man's first thought was to make a trip abroad, to return for a visit to the British Isles, the home of his ancestors and the centre of the full, rich and stimulating life that we imagined went on in the outer world.

Even the very animals we bred were dependent upon periodical return to Europe, for it was soon discovered that horses, cattle and other stock (though not sheep) declined after the third generation unless they were refreshed by new blood brought in from England, Scotland and Ireland. Australia, apart from its gold and its eucalyptus and wattle trees, seemed to contribute nothing of its own.

There was another aspect of our isolation that was less consciously felt but was just as important. We had no history, no past behind us. No invasion or civil war had uprooted Australia during its brief history— the wars were all abroad—and with the exception of the aborigines, no one had ever lived in the country before us. There were no ruins, no relics of past civilizations, no myths, no reassuring sense of the continuity of things.

After the first exploration of the country, the best we could do in the way of local history was the miners' disturbance known as the Eureka Stockade, and the adventures of a young Irish desperado named Ned Kelly. Kelly was a bushranger who robbed banks and pubs in country towns, and he made his last stand against the police in an iron, pipe-like helmet with a slit in it for his eyes. We rather liked Ned Kelly. We felt he expressed some of our own freebooting irritation with authority, our own tough approach to life. We thought we had to be tough, I suspect, partly in order to disguise our inner loneliness.

Nolan, so far as I can see, is bedevilled by none of these misgivings, and this is a fundamental aspect of his work. He accepts the world in which he grew up, he sees the Australian predicament, and it does not distress or embarrass him. Instead he makes a virtue of it. He discovers beauty and legend in places where hardly anyone had looked before; he realizes that no one is really isolated and that the Australian scene is merely a recreation of the ancient past. He seems to be saying that this sense of the past—this myth, this continuous dream—is the thing that explains and animates the human race; or, in other words, the same hates and loves are with us all the time. It is to the painting of this dream that Nolan, with a peculiar concentration and originality—for he imitates no other painter I can think of—has devoted his life.

To comprehend the Kelly paintings one has to know something of the hard, uncompromising nature of the Australian bush as it was when the first settlers arrived. Natural disasters—bush fires, floods and drought—played a great part in our national consciousness in Australia. In a young country, where we had no reserves either of man power or of money, it was an annihilating thing to see your wooden house burned down, your crops swept away by a cloudburst, and your animals die for lack of grass. Drought caused the worst havoc. It was a slow and paralysing business, the sun beating down week after week from a brassy sky, the land turning from green to lifeless brown, the cattle with their protruding ribs, standing listlessly on the open plain; and there was nothing, absolutely nothing, that could be done about it. The stock-rider, with bitterness, grew accustomed to the sight of the white bones of his dead cattle scattered around the dried-up water-hole. This was death in an immensity of space, a ruthless and natural inevitability. But there remained, as Nolan discovered in his drawings, a marvellous abstraction in the skeleton lying on the sand, a suggestion that death, though terrible, was by no means a vile or an ugly thing. There is a mute nobility in the simple pattern of the bones.

With Ned Kelly, Nolan descends from the general disaster to the particular tragedy, from the natural abstraction to the human myth. As

x

bushrangers go, young Kelly (he was only twenty-five when he was finally caught and executed), was a cut above his kind. He made war upon the government rather than upon individuals, and the letter in which he explained his motives to the world is the eloquent and convinced plea of a revolutionary rather than a criminal. Yet a criminal he was; there was no place for him in a settled community, and if we are to consider him sympathetically we must do so on his own terms: as a brave and unrepentant misfit, as the avenger of injustice, as one man defying destiny, as the personification of the poet's idea that an hour of glorious life is worth an age without a name. This I think is Nolan's approach to the Kelly saga. He is on Kelly's side. His haunting, monolithic figure in the iron mask has the flames of hell upon it, but that slit for the eyes is wonderfully expressive of defiance; this is the crisis of a strong man in chaos, and once again the tragedy is beautiful. With his Kelly paintings Nolan began to reach up toward the full range of his special talent, the uninhibited expression of an emotion in paint.

There is something of an Irish rebel in all this, of Brendan Behanism transported to the Antipodes, of slow-burning resentment flaring up into an act of crazy retaliation that has no rhyme or reason in it. Kelly was no Robin Hood. Yet who is to say he was absolutely in the wrong? Men were transported to the colonies for doing no more than steal a sheep or a loaf of bread. The treatment of convicts in prisons like Port Arthur in Tasmania was excessively harsh, and the working man was underprivileged in a way that would be unthinkable today. The police could be very brutal in a manhunt.

Now, it would be going too far to say that Kelly and his gang acted out of a sense of social grievance: they shot down the policemen who came after them for one reason only—to save their own skins—and the more they murdered the more they realized that there was no turning back, no hope for them in civilized society. Yet at the heart of this dilemma which was of their own making there was a genuine *cri du cœur*. For them the times were out of joint, the conditions of life intolerable, and there was only one thing to do with the police who were enforcing the law—to make war against them. Kelly may have begun with a wild and reckless spree of robbery from which he did not know how to extricate himself, but he well may have ended up, as Nolan seems to suggest, as a self-convinced martyr.

Be all this as it may, there is a remarkable sense of the contemporary scene in these paintings. In a moment one is swept back into the days of the helmeted trooper in his white breeches, of the settler's wood-burning stove and the busy Victorian wallpaper, of the wildflowers springing delicately from the dry ground, of the wisps of camp-fire smoke hanging over the bush settlements in the mornings and the evenings, and of the red sunset. These glimpses are a wonderful evocation of the Australian past.

Success—and by success I also mean that sense of fulfillment a creative man has when he knows that he is on the right track and working to the limit of his powers—did not come to Nolan at all easily. From his earliest student days he has never been conventional. His subjects at first were abstract, and his first one-man show was a collection of calligraphic fantasies and collages. One outraged visitor threw a pot of green paint at the exhibits. Nolan has never painted on canvas, but chooses instead a coated and glazed paperboard, glass, or Masonite, and pigments of his own invention, such as an admixture of poster paints and polyvinyl acetate. Even later on, when he turned to studies with a recognizable subject, his paintings were still a long way from what most people thought a painting ought to be. Not surprisingly, it has only been within the past few years that there has been any widespread appreciation or knowledge of the great force and truth of his originality.

He now lives in London, where in addition to his paintings he has produced a spate of other work—book jackets, theatre décor, lithographs —so much of it, indeed, that some of his friends have wondered whether his talents might not suffer from too much expression. But he seems to work with extraordinary facility and extraordinary fidelity; and he himself is such a natural, friendly, unaffected man that it is unlikely that he will be spoiled by the recognition he is now receiving all over the world.

xii

Unlike most artists he travels a great deal. The Arizona desert and the temples of Angkor, India and Italy, the Middle East and the valley of the Lower Nile, all these and many more have drawn him along a Jason-like journey in search of the golden myth. But it is his Australian background that probably moves him most, however cosmopolitan he may have become. He plans once more to return to the outback to study those parched and desiccated forms on the red earth. He has also been working at the illustration of a long, esoteric poem by the Australian Alwyn Lee. It is a nostalgic work about their mutual birthplace, Melbourne, a filtering-through of early memories to a sophisticated present, somewhat in the manner of James Joyce. After all, Nolan *knows* this world of the pubs and the football crowds, of the bush fires and droughts, and of the desperate manhunt through the bush; and he was born just in time to have had a whiff of the early pioneering days when earthen roads came into the heart of the city, and the farmer, returning from market, rode off with his horse and buggy across the endless plain.

In recent years a million immigrants have descended on Australia, atomic piles are being built in the outback, and jet planes are in the sky. The old isolation is over and done with forever. Yet all these changes would be confused and meaningless without a tradition—the continuous racial instinct that reaches out of the past and into the future. Nolan more than any other living artist has observed this tradition and has refreshed and illuminated it by his work.

ALAN MOOREHEAD

NED KELLY

In Max Brown's *Australian Son*, an account of the life of the outlaw Ned Kelly, there is a quotation from Maxim Gorky which helps us to perceive the significance of Sidney Nolan's images of Kelly. "Side by side with the unhappy figure of Faust", wrote Gorky, "stands another character also known to every nation. In Italy he is Pulcinello, in England Punch, in Turkey Karapet, in our country Petruska. He is the invincible hero of the puppet show. He defeats everyone and everybody —the police, the clergy—even death and the devil—while he himself remains immortal. In this crude and naive image the working people incarnated their own selves and their firm belief that in the long run it will be they who will defeat and overcome everything and everybody." The paintings of Ned Kelly which Nolan has made since leaving Australia have some Faustian characteristics, and as Colin MacInnes has so well said, they dignify and redeem "the loss and sorrow of this rare young life", but in Nolan's first Ned Kelly series painted in Australia in 1946-47—the series which concerns us here—Kelly is the invincible and immortal hero of the puppet show; Australia's Petruska.

The attributes of such a figure are implicit in Ned Kelly's character and exploits, but none of the accounts of his life by serious Australian writers has managed to extricate him from the melodramatic atmosphere of the 19th-century illustrations in which the killings at Stringybark Creek and the last stand at Glenrowan were realistically reconstructed. The crude ballads written while Kelly was still alive, which were immensely popular with the underprivileged classes, are nearer to the spirit of Nolan's image than anything that has been written since. In the four lines from a ballad which Nolan quotes as a subtitle to one of the paintings, it's taken for granted that the thinning of the ranks of the police and the robbing of the banks of the landlords is a right and proper occupation for a brave and decent man. Another of these doggerels, *Ballad of the Wombat Ranges*, which was so popular at the time that attempts were made to suppress it, is a totally amoral and gleeful celebration of the killing of the policemen at Stringybark Creek, but nevertheless manages to end with a wonderfully brutal tribute to Kelly's natural goodness:

> But brave Kelly muttered sadly,
> As he loaded up his gun
> "Oh, what a bloody pity
> That the bugger tried to run!"

It is this same implacable hero of the common people, natural scourge of the police and inscrutable image of unqualified rightness, that Nolan has so brilliantly and with so disarming an air of simplicity extricated or rather abstracted from the Kelly story.

His pictorial treatment of the episodes reflects his response, as he himself has remarked, to "Kelly's own words, to Rousseau and to sunlight." To Kelly's own words in particular.

Kelly's naive, passionate, and sometimes comical rhetoric abounds in fierce denunciations and contemptuous descriptions of the police. His 8000-word manifesto known as the Jerilderie Letter because he tried to get it printed there when he "bailed up" the entire township before robbing the bank, is full of such outbursts, ranging from well-argued accusations to this kind of child-like abuse: "A parcel of big, ugly, fat-necked, wombat-headed, big-bellied, magpie-legged, narrow-hipped, splay-footed sons of Irish Bailiffs or English Lords which is better known as officers of Justice or Victoria Police."

In order to create an image of the police that would signify their permanent role as the Enemy and make visible the attributes reluctantly conferred upon the force by the Royal Commission which enquired into the circumstances of the Kelly outbreak in the year following Kelly's execution, including indolence, incompetence, cowardice and brutality,

Nolan had to invent a figurative system which would go beyond appearances without altogether dispensing with them. He found the prototype for such a figuration, as his own reference to Henri Rousseau indicates, in the art of those simple, untrained painters who, in 19th-century New England and 20th-century France, produced stiff, solemn incorrect versions of the human figure oddly and intensely imbued with human presence. The unreal realism of the naive painter is the visual counterpart of Kelly's illiterate eloquence.

The policemen in Nolan's paintings verge on the grotesque. They are rather sinister figures of fun, somewhat reminiscent of the keystone cops, comic but capable of violence. Their heads are slightly too large for their bodies, and the lower part of their bodies tends to dwindle, bringing to mind Kelly's "narrow-hipped, magpie-legged". Their faces are expressionless, their movements stiff and doll-like; when there is more than one of them in a painting, they are scarcely differentiated, and the uniforms give them a communal identity.

When the police were actually tracking Kelly they usually posed as horse-dealers, surveyors or prospectors and were rarely in uniform; but in Nolan's paintings they are never out of uniform, and by the same token, Kelly is never out of his armour, although it was made specifically for a "last stand" and the outlaws donned their metal suits only when they were in their hideouts, where they shot at one another to test the armour's impregnability. The armour was much too heavy and cumbersome for wear on their usual swift comings and goings. But Nolan has created a world of visual ritual, where the meaning of everything seen must be perceived.

The strange and fantastic form which Nolan has given to Kelly could not plausibly have consorted with figures more naturalistically conceived than his policemen; but he is perfectly at home with these stiff, doll-like figures, much as the saints in early Christian pictures are at home with the devils; distinct and apart, but enfolded in the same conception of reality.

The poetic device which identifies Kelly with an inventive abstract version of his home-made armour enables Nolan to achieve so effective an interplay of spectral apparition and human presence that Kelly's invincibility and immortality are self-evident. In its most radical aspect, this device is simply a black, flat, paper-thin silhouette, without front or back, and with a slot in the headpiece which reveals instead of human eyes a prospect of flat, lonely, interminable landscape. It is always the most sharply visible thing in the painting, uncannily alive but untouchable and invulnerable.

Curiously enough, in providing his figures with an appropriate landscape setting, he has not had to resort to those disruptions of scale which occur in the paintings of the modern primitives, but has been able to rely upon his sense of the "otherness" of the Australian scene. They are straightforward topographical landscapes, faithful to what is seen, but seen from some way off, rarely detailed, and somewhat dream-like in their remoteness, as if a traveller making his way towards them might always find himself at exactly the same distance from them. Usually the horizon line goes straight across the middle of the painting, and on one side of it there is a golden, sunlit emptiness and on the other a blueness faded a little by the light. Kelly and the policemen are the fauna of the sunlit emptiness, no more surprising and no less undeniable than the kangaroo.

It is not surprising that Nolan had a period of abstract experiment before painting his first Kelly series, for there is a sense in which the form he devised for the Kelly figure is now independent of the contexts he provided for it. It has so basic a simplicity that it can now be drawn by anyone. Diagramatically, it is almost as simple as the cross, and even more simple than the swastika because its relationship to the human head on a human neck means that it can't be drawn the wrong way round and could only wilfully be drawn upside down. It has the formal self-sufficiency of the cross and the swastika, and as a sign remains as close to the thing signified as the Cross to the Crucifixion. Nolan himself has already explored many of its possibilities in terms of the Cross/Crucifixion relationship, for it can take on substance whenever he pleases. As a symbolic personage, it is probably more broadly communicative than any other example in modern art. Perhaps in this respect the nearest images to it are Moore's woman-mountain and Picasso's Minotaur, but these remain much more dependent upon their creators. Moore and Picasso have given the woman-mountain and the Minotaur a fabulous formal range, and they are both great masters of simplification: but neither image has yielded up its essence in a diagram. It's evident, I think, that Nolan's Ned Kelly could be the hero of comic strips and cartoon films without further intervention on the part of the artist. It is only because it has remained within the confines of the art of painting that it is not one of the familiar characters of popular art.

The Kelly device already carries a great weight of association for the people of one nation and for very many people outside Australia who are familiar with Nolan's work, and it might yet be chalked on the walls of all the cities of the world as a sign for Freedom.

In the notes which follow the plates, I have attempted to provide some sense of the mass of factual material from which Nolan has elicited his legendary figure.

The quotations under the titles of the pictures were extracted by the painter from the Royal Commission's report of 1881, from newspapers and from J. J. Kenneally's *The Inner History of the Kelly Gang*.

ROBERT MELVILLE

1   LANDSCAPE

2   NED KELLY

3 THE BURNING TREE

4   CONSTABLE FITZPATRICK AND KATE KELLY

MORNING CAMP

6   FIRST CLASS MARKSMAN

7　MANSFIELD

8   STEVE HART DRESSED AS A GIRL

9   QUILTING THE ARMOUR

10 DEATH OF
CONSTABLE SCANLON

11 STRINGYBARK
CREEK

12 DEATH OF
SERGEANT KENNEDY

13   THE WATCH TOWER

14   THE ALARM

15   THE PURSUIT

6   THE ENCOUNTER

17   THE MARRIAGE OF AARON SHERRITT

18   THE DEFENCE OF AARON SHERRITT

19   THE EVENING

20   BUSH PICNIC

21   THE QUESTIONING

22   THE SLIP

3 MRS REARDON AT GLENROWAN

24   SIEGE AT GLENROWAN

25   BURNING AT GLENROWAN

27   THE TRIAL

1 LANDSCAPE

The "Kelly Country" is that portion of north-eastern Victoria which extends from Mansfield in the south to Yarrawonga in the north, and from Euroa in the south-east to Tallangatta in the north-west.

It was in the bushland of colonial Victoria that a group of painters produced the first Australian landscapes which were not tied to European academic conventions, and their "blue and gold" impressionism is still a greatly prized aspect of Australia's cultural heritage. The leaders of the group were Tom Roberts, Arthur Streeton, Frederick McCubbin and Charles Condor, who later made a name for himself in Europe. They began to paint in the bush three or four years after Kelly's death. Their impressionism was not a direct offshoot of the art of the French Impressionists, which was unknown to them, and although they called themselves Impressionists they took the name from an innocuous remark of Gerôme's to his students, to the effect that the first thing to look for in a painting is the general impression of colour. No painters have ever been more devoted to the open air: they often worked as a community, and in a land "three quarters of the year in sunlight" spent many months at a time in the bush. Their feeling for Victoria's golden, sun-drenched earth and heat-hazed blue skies was accompanied by a sense of solidarity with the people who earned their living off the land, and their landscapes usually included people at work—stockmen, shearers, waggoners, "selectors" felling trees on their small strips of land, or rambling men sitting by lonely littles fires. McCubbin painted a "bush burial", which was the kind of burial Ned Kelly's father was given. "Red" Kelly, as he was called, died at the age of forty-seven on his little dairy farm at a place called Avenal, leaving a widow and seven children. Friends

39

helped to make the coffin, and as there was no priest in the area a neighbour read the service. Ned, who was eleven years old and the eldest child, registered his father's death with the police because his mother could not read or write.

It was the time of a fierce struggle for land between the licensed and well set-up landowners called squatters and the "selectors" who were attempting to break the squatters' monopoly of Crown lands. The Land Act of 1865, one of the results of the Eureka Stockade protest, entitled a selector to occupy an area of twenty acres for three years at an annual rent of two shillings an acre, and if at the end of three years the selector had improved the value of the land by one pound an acre he was entitled to buy the freehold at that price. The squatters often got round the Act by putting their own hirelings on selections and buying the freehold as soon as it was granted. As the privileged and property-owning class, the squatters had the police pretty well in their pockets and were assured of their helpful intervention when making complaints about selectors.

A few months after "Red" Kelly died, his widow with the help of her father and brothers, the Quinn family, who were themselves selectors, acquired a twenty-acre selection on Eleven Mile Creek, a few miles from her father's selection at Glenmore.

2 NED KELLY

We rob their banks
We thin their ranks
And ask no thanks
For what we do.

When Ned Kelly was fifteen years old a hawker accused him of borrowing his horse without permission. After an argument Ned knocked the hawker down and later sent the hawker's wife a parcel containing a calf's testicles. The hawker complained to the police and

Ned was sent to prison for three months for assault and indecent behaviour. Three weeks after he came out he was in front of the magistrate again on a charge of stealing a thoroughbred mare and resisting arrest. This time he was sent to prison for three years, but the sentence was reduced by six months for good behaviour. He then worked for two years as a timber cutter and station hand on estates in the Wombat Ranges, but in 1877 he gave up regular work to go prospecting on the upper reaches of the King River. His period of prospecting coincided with frequent reports of the loss of valuable horses and stock by squatters in the area. The police were reinforced and Ned was persistently questioned by them about his movements. In the Jerilderie Letter, he wrote, "I began to think they wanted me to give them something to talk about. Therefore I started wholesale and retail horse and cattle dealing..." He maintained that the police were always impounding horses that belonged to poor selectors on the pretext that they had found them on squatters' land; the selectors had to pay a fine before they could get their horses back and sometimes they didn't have the money to pay. Kelly was an expert at changing the brands on horses, and he was in New South Wales with a string of re-branded horses, for which he was paid full market value, when the Victoria police finally issued a warrant for his arrest. A few days later another warrant was issued for the arrest of his younger brother Dan on a similar charge, and it was Constable Fitzpatrick's attempt to arrest Dan at his mother's home, without being able to prove that a warrant had been issued, that started the train of events that turned the brothers into outlaws.

3 THE BURNING TREE

At one time during a police search in the Warby Ranges I allowed the men, seeing they had no warmth for weeks, to set fire to an old hollow tree.

Kate, in the exercise of her domestic duties, was passing by Fitzpatrick when the latter seized her and pulled her onto his knee.

Constable Fitzpatrick was a frequent if unwelcome visitor at the Kelly home. Ned Kelly declared that he had heard from another policeman that Fitzpatrick had sold his own sister to a Chinese, and Ned himself thought that the deceit and cowardice were "too plain to be seen in the puny cabbage hearted looking face". Ultimately, he was dismissed from the force as a "person of indifferent character, untrustworthy and incapable of carrying out his duties".

There was no substance in the charge that Dan Kelly had stolen a horse, and the warrant was issued as part of a deliberate policy of harrassing and persecuting the Kellys and the Quinns to try to force them to move out of the territory. The police considered them to be trouble-makers.

Fitzpatrick had been drinking before he called at Eleven Mile Creek with the idea of arresting Dan. He was probably a bit fuddled, for he had had no instructions to call at the Kelly home and was supposed to be on his way to Greta township to relieve a constable at the station there. When Fitzpatrick told Dan that he had come to take him in, Dan said he was prepared to go with him to clear himself of the charge but hadn't eaten all day and would have to have a meal first. Fitzpatrick followed Dan into the house, and Mrs Kelly asked to see the warrant and was very angry when he tapped his revolver and said, "This is my warrant". She picked up the fire shovel and brandished it in Fitzpatrick's face and is supposed to have said, "If my son Ned was here, he would ram that revolver down your throat". By then, darkness was coming on, and two bush workers who had arranged to have a meal at the Kellys came into the yard. Dan remarked jokingly, "Here's Ned coming now". The remark startled the constable. He pulled out his revolver and peered into the darkness, and Dan, thinking that he might start shooting out of nervousness, snatched the revolver and, using a wrestling hold known as "Heenan's hug", threw him to the floor. Fitzpatrick struck his wrist against the door catch as he fell, tearing the skin, and he lay on the floor as if in a faint. Feeling that things had taken an unfortunate turn, the Kellys and the two bush workers were very anxious to put things right. They bandaged his wrist and gave him a glass of brandy. He for his part, conscious no doubt of being unarmed and of being physically no match for Dan, suddenly became friendly and admitted that it was only an accident. He ate a hearty meal with the family and joked and drank with them until about eleven o'clock. As he was leaving, he even advised Dan to clear out into the bush before someone appeared with the warrant.

Instead of riding on to Greta, where he was long overdue, he started back for Benalla, where he had come from, but stopped on the way at the same pub that he had visited before going to the Kellys, and he didn't get back to Benalla police station until two in the morning. On the way, he worked out a feverish and mischievous excuse for not going to Greta and to explain his bandaged wrist and semi-intoxicated state. His superiors knew him to be unreliable, and they would certainly have treated his story with suspicion if they had not been intent on making things bad for the Kellys. He claimed that in attempting to pick up Dan Kelly in the course of his duty he had been attacked by Ned Kelly and two other men, all armed with revolvers, and that by a trick Dan Kelly had got possession of his own. Thus unarmed, he was faced by four armed men and a woman with a fire shovel. Having the unarmed constable entirely at his mercy, Ned had then tried unsuccessfully to murder him. He shot at him twice from a distance of five feet, but missed him, so the woman had hit him over the head with the shovel. As he tried to ward off the blow, Ned fired a third time, and managed to hit him in the wrist. He fell stunned to the floor and when he came round he found that they had seated him on a chair and were preparing to take the bullet out of his wrist, which had lodged just beneath the skin, making only a flesh wound. He refused to let them take out the bullet and courageously removed it himself with his penknife. They kept him a prisoner for several hours and only released him after forcing him to swear that he would not report the shooting.

Warrants were immediately issued for the arrest of Ned on the charge of wounding with intent to murder and for the arrest of Mrs Kelly, Dan and the two other men as accessories. One of the men was wrongly named as William Skillion, the husband of Ned's favourite sister Maggie. He was at the house of a horse-dealer at the time of the scuffle.

Ned was in New South Wales and didn't hear of the affair until several days later. Dan had taken to the bush. The other three were not expecting arrest and were taken separately. Mrs Kelly was still suckling her youngest child by her second husband, and took the child with her. There were now no menfolk at the Kelly home, and Maggie Skillion went to live there, and help with the three youngest children. The police raided the house continually in the hope of catching Ned and Dan by surprise. Ned gives a bitter description of their conduct: "I heard how they used to rush into the house, upset all the milk-dishes, break tins of eggs, empty the flour out of the bags onto the ground, and even the meat out of the cask, and destroy all the provisions. They would shove the girls in front of them into the rooms like dogs, so that if anyone was there, they would shoot the girls first. But they knew well I was not there, or I would have scattered their blood and brains like rain and manured the Eleven Mile Creek with their bloated carcases—and yet remember there is not one drop of murderous blood in my veins!"

He came back from New South Wales when he heard of his mother's arrest, and found Dan in hiding in a lonely gully in the Wombat Ranges. Among those who knew where Dan was hiding were his friends Steve Hart and Joe Byrne, who were soon to become the other two members of the Kelly gang. Ned's first move was to inform the magistrates that he and his brother would give themselves up on condi-

44

tion that the charge against their mother was withdrawn, but the magistrates made only a vague and worthless promise that if they gave themselves up they would "use their endeavours to carry out the conditions they wished to impose".

When Mrs Kelly and the other two prisoners were tried before Judge Sir Redmond Barry, only two witnesses were called for the defence. They gave evidence that Skillion was with them at the time of the alleged shooting, but the alibi was brushed aside, and all three were found guilty. Before passing sentence, Judge Barry said to Mrs Kelly, "If your son Ned were here, I would make an example of him! I would give him a sentence of fifteen years." Then he sentenced Mrs Kelly to three years and each of the two men to six years' imprisonment. Ned's response to these harsh sentences was fierce and vivid. "The police got great credit and praise in the papers for arresting the mother of twelve children—one an infant on her breast—and those two quiet, hard-working, innocent men, who would not know the difference between a revolver and a saucepanhandle. They were kept six months awaiting trial, and then convicted on the evidence of the meanest article that ever the sun shone on. It will pay the Government to give justice and liberty to those people who are suffering innocently. If not, I will be compelled to show some colonial stratagem which will open the eyes of not only the police and inhabitants of Victoria, but also the whole British Army. They will have to acknowledge that their hounds were barking at the wrong stump, and that Fitzpatrick will be the cause of greater slaughter to the Union Jack than Saint Patrick was to the snakes and toads of Ireland."

Ned and Dan Kelly were now well aware that the police would probably shoot to kill. They heard from their friends that the police were boasting that they would "blow them to pieces" and "shoot them like dogs". Three days after Mrs Kelly started her sentence, eight mounted police, divided into two parties, set out for the Wombat Ranges, where the two Kellys were reported to be hiding. The party in charge of Sergeant Kennedy made its camp at Stringybark Creek.

5 Morning Camp

Ned Kelly knew all our camps in the Warby Ranges. He would describe the constables who used to go and look for the horses at daylight, and the one who was told off to light the fire and boil the billy of tea.

6 First class Marksman

Confined to the mountains, the four members of the band practised so constantly with shotguns and revolvers that they all became first class marksmen.

7 Mansfield

In the township of Mansfield there is a monument to the three policemen killed at Stringybark Creek, and three headstones in the churchyard. It was to this township on a quiet Sunday afternoon that a man from an outlying homestead brought constable McIntyre, the only survivor of the ambush, with the news of the shooting. That same evening, two policemen, a doctor and five civilians with borrowed firearms and two pack horses returned with McIntyre to Stringybark Creek to bring back the bodies of constables Lonigan and Scanlon. They reached it soon after midnight and found the two dead constables where they had been shot down. They surveyed the scene by the light of matches. The tent had been burned down and all the camping gear taken away. There was no sign of Sergeant Kennedy so they waited uneasily until daybreak before continuing the search, but when the light came they were frightened that the Kelly gang might return. McIntyre, who had fled while the gun battle was still going on, had told them that he thought Kennedy had surrendered, and after making a hasty search along the creek the party decided that he must have done so, and hurried back to Mansfield with the bodies of

Lonigan and Scanlon strapped to the pack horses. Further search parties were sent out, with police reinforcements from other districts, and on the following Thursday a farmer found the body of Kennedy in the scrub where Kelly had left him. There were wounds in his chest, and the police said that one of his ears had been cut off.

A Felons Apprehension Bill was rushed through by the Government, giving civilians the right to shoot any member of the gang on sight, and the police power to arrest anyone suspected of harbouring or assisting them, and a reward was offered of £500 for each man, dead or alive.

8   STEVE HART DRESSED AS A GIRL

He appears to have been possessed of a considerable courage and resource, and during the period of his outlawry frequently rode about in feminine attire.

Steve Hart was Dan Kelly's closest friend, and was only twenty-two when he died at Glenrowan. His father had a small farm on the outskirts of Wangaratta. Steve, like Dan, was much more slightly built than Ned, but he was reputed to be the best horseman in north-eastern Victoria. He and Joe Byrne threw in their lot with Ned and Dan after what amounted to Ned's declaration of war on the police. Until the Stringybark affair, the police thought that the Kellys were on their own, and even after they discovered that there were four members of the gang, it was some time before the other two were identified. It gave Hart and Byrne more freedom of movement than the Kellys, and it was Steve Hart who went into the township of Euroa to size it up before the gang raided the bank.

Joe Byrne, two years older than Hart, was the son of a gold-miner and lived in the Woolshed diggings near Beechworth. He was tall and handsome and very self-confident. He could shatter a coin thrown into the air with one shot and move like a ghost in the bush. Before Joe joined the Kelly gang his best friend had been Aaron Sherritt.

Sherritt's father had been a policeman before taking up farming, and the Kellys never trusted him. It may well have been the fact that he never found favour with the Kellys that caused him to become a police spy. He had immense admiration for Ned Kelly, and once said to a police official who paid him for information about the Kellys, "I am a better man than Joe Byrne, or Dan Kelly, or Steve Hart, but I look upon Ned Kelly as an extraordinary man. There is no man in the world like him; he is superhuman; he is invincible, and you can do nothing with him".

There would have been a fifth member of the gang if Jim Kelly, the youngest of the brothers, had not been serving a jail sentence for horse-stealing.

9 QUILTING THE ARMOUR

Mrs Skillion, who was Margaret Kelly, sat out in the evenings sewing the soft blue quilting into the headpiece of the armour.

Early in 1880, the police received reports that a number of mouldboards of ploughs had been stolen from farms in the neighbourhood of Greta. Search parties and black-trackers were sent to investigate, and the trackers found the marks of high-heeled riding boots on the farms, and it was known that the Kellys wore such boots.

At a hideout in the Greta swamps the gang heated the mouldboards and shaped them round a log. Each suit of armour consisted of three main sections: a front section to cover the chest and stomach, a back section to protect most of the spine, and a kind of apron which was fastened to the front section by a swivel, which protected the thighs and could be used on a horse. The front and back sections were held together at the sides by leather laces and supported by leather straps over the shoulders. Ned's helmet was shaped to go round the head and cover the nape of the neck; between the two hinged front pieces there was a slit for the eyes. His head was protected from the iron by a thick woollen skull cap. There was no protection for the arms and legs.

The gang made the armour because Ned was convinced that the Queensland black-trackers would eventually lead the police to their last hideout and that they would be surrounded by a big force of police. He hoped that the armour would resist heavy fire.

10   Death of Constable Scanlon

He was in the act of firing again when Ned Kelly fired and Scanlon fell from his horse and died almost immediately.

When Sergeant Kennedy's party set up camp at Stringybark Creek, the Kellys were in a hideout little more than a mile away and they quickly realized that a party of police was in the vicinity. The morning after setting up camp, Kennedy and Scanlon rode into the bush, leaving McIntyre to bake some bread and prepare the evening meal and Lonigan to look after the horses. McIntyre with almost unbelievable stupidity spent part of the morning shooting at parrots with a shotgun and in the afternoon lit a big fire to cook the evening meal. Either of these activities would have been enough to pin-point the whereabouts of the camp. The Kellys kept it under close observation until the middle of the afternoon, then moved in on McIntyre and Lonigan. Leaving Byrne and Hart in the shadows, the two brothers walked into the clearing, shouting "Bail up!"

McIntyre raised his hands, but Lonigan dived behind a pile of logs and reached for his revolver. Ned shot him through the forehead. Ned then asked McIntyre if anyone was in the tent, and McIntyre told him that Kennedy and Scanlon had gone on a long expedition and wouldn't be back that night. Ned set his three companions to watch the approaches to the camp and waited by the campfire with McIntyre. He told the constable that he didn't shoot anyone who held up his hands, and promised McIntyre that he would spare his life and the lives of Kennedy and Scanlon if he would persuade them to surrender without a fight. It was dusk when they returned to the camp, and under Kelly's instructions McIntyre called out to them, "Halt and surrender—you're surrounded". Scanlon wheeled his horse and fired immediately at Ned, who responded with a shot that hit Scanlon in the chest, and the policeman tumbled dead from his horse. Kennedy had already dismounted, and he aimed shots at both Dan and Ned. As he dodged behind a tree, McIntyre seized his chance and jumped on Kennedy's horse and made his escape. Stalking Kennedy from tree to tree, Ned hit him with a shotgun charge in the right armpit and as he attemped to run pulled out Lonigan's revolver and shot him in the chest. Ned stood over him for a time in silence, as if lost in thought, then shot him through the heart.

11 STRINGYBARK CREEK

"If left alive Kennedy would", Kelly said, "be left to a slow, torturing death at the mercy of ants, flies and the packs of dingoes." Therefore he decided to put an end to the sufferings of the wounded sergeant, and, as the latter momentarily turned his head, Kelly fired and shot him through the heart.

The movements of the outlaws would have been severely restricted if they had taken prisoners; they certainly couldn't do anything effective for a seriously wounded man. The police said that when they found the body one of the ears had been cut off, but it is more likely that they told this story to blacken Kelly's name, and put the common people against him. There is no evidence that Kelly ever subjected a human being to brutal treatment.

Kelly: *"I put his cloak over him and left him as well as I could and were they my own brothers I couldn't have been more sorry for them.   This cannot be called wilful murder for I was compelled to shoot them, or lie down and let them shoot me."*

13   THE WATCH TOWER

From the tower, which we mounted in shifts, a good view could be had of the town in all directions, and in particular of the roads by which we might expect the outlaws to arrive.

Feverish precautions were taken in some of the townships after the Kellys had successfully raided the banks in Euroa and Jerilderie, taking several thousand pounds and burning many documents connected with the debts of small farmers.

14   THE ALARM

A peacock which used to sleep on the top of a tin shed.   The bird was accustomed to making warning cries at the approach of any stranger.

The peacock was at the homestead of the Quinns—Ned's aunts and uncles—at Glenmore.   The bushranger Harry Power had his hideout about a mile from the house and was supplied with provisions by the Quinns.   It was noticed by some of the people who were "bailed up" on the roads by Power that he was accompanied by a youth who kept a look-out at some distance from the hold-up, and it is thought that Ned, only fifteen years old at that time, had been persuaded by the Quinns to take the job of Power's "off-sider".   He was arrested on suspicion, but after being held on remand for a month was released because the police failed to produce evidence.

The police finally took Power in his hideout. They were led there by an informer, going by night so that they wouldn't be noticed by the peacock, whose shrill cries would have set all the dogs barking. Power thought that it was Ned who had given him away, but the reward money was paid to Jack Lloyd, who was married to one of the Quinn sisters. The money was actually handed to him by one of the squatters, so that the suspicions of the Quinn family would not be roused. They were not the kind to appreciate informers.

When Power was caught, the newspapers called him "the last of the bushrangers", and in a sense it was true, because although the Kellys were later to stage more daring hold-ups, their activities were more in the nature of an insurrection.

15 THE PURSUIT

I am sure the police would not ride them down in a day; they would have to hunt them down, but not ride them down—the outlaws were well mounted.

The Kelly gang had better horses than the police; probably the best that the squatters could breed. They were justly proud of their horsemanship and after their successful raid on Euroa they entertained their temporary prisoners with a display of trick riding.

16 THE ENCOUNTER

Should a constable encounter one of these outlaws, he should apprehend him with the maximum efficiency and devotion to duty.

17 THE MARRIAGE OF AARON SHERRITT

We police regarded him as a valuable and cunning spy. He got married on Boxing Day, 1879. Constable Barry was at the time in charge of the search party hidden in the cave. After his marriage we regarded him as less trustworthy.

A police Superintendent described Sherritt thus: "He was a remarkable looking man. If he had walked down Collins Street, everyone would have stared at him. His walk, his appearance and everything else was remarkable. He was a man of most wonderful endurance. He would go night after night without sleep in the coldest nights in winter. He would be under a tree in his shirtsleeves, without any blanket of any kind, while my men were wrapped up in furs, in the middle of the winter."

He told the police to watch the home of Joe Byrne's mother at Woolshed, and they established a police camp in a small cave on a rocky hill overlooking the Byrne property. At about this time, Sherritt became engaged to Joe Byrne's sister and he used some of the money given to him by the police to buy her a horse. He regularly contacted the police in the cave at night, and when Mrs Byrne was collecting firewood one night near the cave she saw them together. Sherritt, seeing that she had recognized him, said to the police, "I'm a dead man."

The first result of Mrs Byrne's visit to the cave was that her daughter broke off her engagement, and exchanged the horse Sherritt had given her for another. Sherritt must have been a pretty cool customer, for he demanded the horse back, and when he was told that it had been swapped he stole the one that was now in her possession, and sold it. Mrs Byrne then went to the police station and demanded Sherritt's arrest for horse-stealing. The police had to charge him, but brought him in not guilty. Sherritt then married the fifteen-year-old daughter of a Mrs Barry who lived in Woolshed. But it was clear that his life was in danger, and four policemen were secretly lodged with him for protection and actually stayed for six months in the Sherritt's two-roomed hut on his selection, remaining indoors throughout the day and going out at night to watch Mrs Byrne's house.

Mrs Sherritt: "They [the police] were in that position when Dan Kelly came into the room. I was put under the bed. Constable Dowling pulled me down, and then Armstrong caught hold of me, and the two of them shoved me under."

The title is ironical. The police displayed conspicuous cowardice on the night of Sherritt's execution by the Kelly gang for informing.

When the gang had their first conclusive evidence that Sherritt was a police informer, his old friend Joe Byrne wanted to settle with him straightaway and suggested that the police in the cave should be dealt with at the same time. But Ned considered that it would expose them to unnecessary risks to kill Sherritt and the police party unless it was part of a constructive plan. The Queensland black-trackers were making life difficult for the Kellys. Over the months, they had been slowly discovering one hideout after another and putting it out of bounds for the gang, and the area in which the Kellys could move freely about was becoming more and more restricted. They were now confined to a dense and almost impenetrable area of bushland. The money from the bank raids was running out and it was difficult to obtain provisions and information. It was in fact quite evident to Ned that it was only the bad relations between the Queensland black-trackers and the Victoria police that was postponing the inevitable show-down. He decided that the best thing to do was to attempt a break-out so daring that if it came off it would seem that the gang was indestructible.

The plan was brilliant. They would make it clear to the authorities that they were in the vicinity of Woolshed by striking down Sherritt. The automatic response of the police would be to send a trainload of reinforcements from Benalla to Beechworth, the nearest station to Woolshed, and the gang would meanwhile move rapidly out of the district and take over the railway station at Glenrowan, not far from Benalla. There they would tear up part of the track and wreck the train.

54

On the evening of Saturday, 26th June, 1880, Sherritt, his young wife, her mother, who was paying them a call, and constable Duross in plain clothes were sitting by a log fire in the living room and the other three constables were lying down in the unlighted bedroom. At about quarter to seven there was a knock on the back door and constable Duross ran into the bedroom. A German digger who was well-known to the Sherritts called out that he had lost his way. He only lived a quarter of a mile away, and the Sherritts took it for granted that he was drunk. Sherritt opened the door, and saw that the digger was handcuffed. Joe Byrne, standing beside the digger, shot Sherritt twice and he fell dead. Byrne assured the women that he wouldn't harm them but told them to tell the men in the bedroom to come out. There was no move or sound from the four policemen. Joe and Dan stayed outside in the darkness. They had an hour or two on their hands before starting at the pre-arranged time for Glenrowan. It was not part of the plan to kill the policemen in the bedroom; it was in fact necessary that at least one of them should be alive to sound the alarm and telegraph to Benalla for reinforcements. Fearing that the police would start shooting at any moment, the girl offered to go back into the house and tell them to surrender. But when she went to the bedroom door, the policemen grabbed her and pushed her under the bed, no doubt thinking that her presence would be some sort of protection for them, especially as it was well known that the gang had never harmed a woman.

Joe and Dan amused themselves by stacking brushwood against the hut and pretending to set light to it, but the men in the bedroom stayed quiet and at about nine o'clock Joe and Dan departed for their ride to Glenrowan, without letting it be known to the police that they were going.

The police remained in the bedroom all night, and were so thoroughly scared that it was mid-morning before one of them ventured out to walk the eight miles to the police station at Beechworth. He made his way very carefully, fearing that he would be intercepted and it was after mid-day before news of the outrage was telegraphed to Benalla.

The cowardice of the police played havoc with Ned's time-table. He was expecting the news to reach Benalla by midnight at the latest, and the train carrying reinforcements to be at Glenrowan early Sunday morning. It did not arrive until late the following night.

19   THE EVENING

At times, when the troopers and black-trackers had made camp, I would ride ahead in the evening; thinking perhaps to find some clue to the outlaws' movements by travelling alone.

20   BUSH PICNIC

On one occasion the outlaws had arranged to have a picnic some distance from Violet Town. The Kellys' friends flattered the constable and shouted freely for him. He got pretty full, and someone suggested dancing on the green. Good music was available and Ned Kelly took the merry constable as his partner i. a buck set.

21   THE QUESTIONING

The troopers enquired at the homestead as to the whereabouts of the outlaws, but were told to ask the old man who was up bathing himself in the dam.

22   THE SLIP

The gully was exceedingly rough and precipitous. So much so that on one occasion as we were descending in single file one of the pack horses lost its footing and fell.

I came into the yard and screamed for the police to have mercy on me. "I am only a woman; allow me to escape with my children. The outlaws will not interfere with us—do not you."

Kelly had planned to de-rail the train carrying police and black-trackers from Benalla, and then descend on Benalla and obtain fresh funds there before returning to the ranges. There was even a vague idea of taking hostages, to force the authorities to release Mrs Kelly. But the whole day went by at Glenrowan without the train turning up, and it was difficult to hold all the people of Glenrowan in the hotel indefinitely, and Ned sent some people home under thre threat of death if they attemped to get into touch with the outside world. Among them was the school teacher, who decided to take his courage in both hands and wait beyond the bend where the line had been cut, in order to warn the driver of the train.

At night there were singing and dancing in the hotel, and the Kellys, fearing that the police had somehow got wind of their plans and might be coming from a different direction, prepared to leave. Then they heard the train steaming slowly into the station. At this point, knowing that the plan had failed, the outlaws could still have got away. But Ned decided that they would stay and fight. They put on their armour, but they were soon to discover that it hindered their movements and spoilt their aim. Ned said afterwards that "a man gets tired of being hunted like a dog in his native land. I wanted to see the thing end." It had never been Ned's intention to make a stand inside the hotel. But the heavy firing of the police forced Ned's three companions inside, and Ned himself worked his way round to the back of the hotel, with the idea of taking the police from the rear. But he was wounded and lay unconscious for some hours in a field, while the police fired continually at the hotel.

Mrs Reardon was the wife of one of the platelayers who were forced by the Kellys to tear up part of the railway line. Ned's companions were willing to release all the people in the hotel, but the police wouldn't stop firing. Mrs Reardon thought they would hold their fire if she walked out with her baby in her arms. But the police seemed to be in a state bordering on hysteria, and one of them called out that it was Dan Kelly in disguise and shot at her and a bullet went through the baby's shawl.

24 SIEGE AT GLENROWAN

At about eight o'clock in the morning, a heart-rending wail of grief ascended from the hotel. The voice was easily distinguished as that of Mrs Jones, the landlady. Mrs Jones was lamenting the fate of her son, who had been shot in the back by the police, as she supposed fatally. She came out of the hotel crying bitterly and wandered into the bush on several occasions, etc.

Mrs Jones was not trusted by the Kellys. She acted as if she were on their side, but was thought to be no less forthcoming with the police. Mrs Reardon, the platelayer's wife, said in her evidence to the Royal Commission that Mrs Jones's daughter kept her eye on the women and children in the hotel, reckoning where they were and counting them with a revolver in her hand.

25 BURNING AT GLENROWAN

I got no answer, of course, and I looked in and found the bodies of Dan Kelly and Steve Hart lying together. As far as I could tell they were burnt from the waist up. VERY REV. DEAN GIBNEY

The Rev. Matthew Gibney, who became Vicar-General of the Roman Catholic Church in Western Australia, was present most of the day at the seige, and at one time asked permission to go to the hotel and induce the Kellys to surrender, saying that they would not shoot if they knew he was a priest. But he was told that they would not take time to think and would certainly shoot. He said that at no time did the police make an offer of a truce, and that they didn't appear to be under anyone's guidance but simply fired incessantly at the house before finally deciding to set fire to it.

26 GLENROWAN

"Such is Life."

The subtitle quotes Kelly's last words, spoken on the scaffold. The testimony of the railway guard who was on the scene when Ned Kelly regained consciousness, after lying unnoticed in a field for several hours, and walked slowly in his armour towards the police, firing as he came, vividly conveys the atmosphere of apprehension and confusion which prevailed throughout the seige: "I turned round and saw this strange-looking object coming over the hill from the Wangaratta side... It was getting light, but the smoke of the guns hung over the ground and made like a fog... It looked like a great big black fellow. I called out. I said, 'Healey, what's coming?' and somebody behind said 'Keep back, keep back', but the object kept coming on... a man ran away after firing at him, but the thought struck me it was hardly any disgrace to be afeard, because it was not any use firing at him. I knew I was hitting him myself; it did not do any good... I never heard a word about any armour or anything else, not till we were at the log when we pulled it off, because he had like a white mackintosh over the whole affair down to his heels, and the helmet standing on his head, and what with the fog and one thing and another it made him about nine feet high; upon my word it did, coming through the gloom there. I said it was Old Nick, and upon my word I thought it was at the time. I don't believe anyone knew it was Ned Kelly till the helmet came off."

Judge Barry then passed sentence of death, and concluded with the usual formula, "May the Lord have mercy on your soul".   Ned Kelly: "Yes, I will meet you there."

It was decided to try Kelly on the charge of having murdered constables Lonigan and Scanlon at Stringybark Creek.   No witnesses were called for the defence.   The defending counsel, appointed by the Crown because Ned had no funds, relied on an address to the jury, pointing out a few discrepancies in the evidence.

When the Judge asked Kelly if he had anything to say before sentence was passed, Kelly replied: "It is rather too late for me to speak now... Nobody knew about my case except myself and I wish I had insisted on being allowed to examine the witnesses myself... If I had examined the witnesses, I could have thrown a different light on the case.   I do not fear death.   I fear it as little as to drink a cup of tea.   I lay blame on myself that I did not get up yesterday and examine the witnesses, but I thought that if I did so, it would look like bravado and flashness."